GOAT:
Women in Sports

T0191337

Diana Taurasi
≈ Basketball GOAT ≈

HOT TOPICS

Gareth Stevens
PUBLISHING

BY KRISTEN RAJCZAK NELSON

Please visit our website, www.garethstevens.com. For a free color catalog of all our high-quality books, call toll free 1-800-542-2595 or fax 1-877-542-2596.

Library of Congress Cataloging-in-Publication Data
Names: Rajczak Nelson, Kristen, author.
Title: Diana Taurasi : basketball GOAT / Kristen Rajczak Nelson.
Other titles: Basketball greatest of all time
Description: Buffalo, New York : Gareth Stevens Publishing, [2025] |
    Series: GOAT : Women in sports | Includes bibliographical references and
    index.
Identifiers: LCCN 2023028162 | ISBN 9781538293652 (library binding) | ISBN
    9781538293645 (paperback) | ISBN 9781538293669 (ebook)
Subjects: LCSH: Taurasi, Diana–Juvenile literature. | Women basketball
    players–United States–Biography–Juvenile literature. | Women Olympic
    athletes–United States–Biography–Juvenile literature. | Women
    athletes–United States–Biography–Juvenile literature. | Connecticut
    Huskies (Basketball team)–Juvenile literature. | Phoenix Mercury
    (Basketball team)–Juvenile literature. | Women's National Basketball
    Association–Juvenile literature.
Classification: LCC GV884.T377 R35 2025 | DDC 796.323092
    [B]–dc23/eng/20230711
LC record available at https://lccn.loc.gov/2023028162

First Edition

Published in 2025 by
Gareth Stevens Publishing
2544 Clinton St
Buffalo, NY 14224

Designer: Leslie Taylor
Editor: Kristen Rajczak Nelson

Photo credits: Cover (photo) Cal Sport Media/Alamy.com, (wreath) Igoron_vector_3D_render/Shutterstock.com, (banner, cover & series background) RETHELD DESIGN IRI/Shutterstock.com, (basketball icon) Invision Frame/Shutterstockcom; pp. 5, 27 Keeton Gale/Shutterstock.com; p. 7 Lorie Shaull/https://commons.wikimedia.org/wiki/File:Diana_Taurasi_2.jpgs; p. 9 Saw2th/https://commons.wikimedia.org/wiki/File:Taurasi_finale_7977555112_8c929ae012_o.jpg; p. 11 Focus Photography/Shutterstock.com; pp. 13, 17 (right) Zuma Press, Inc./Alamy.com; p. 15 DPPI Media/Alamy.com; p. 17 (left) Abaca Press/Alamy.com; pp. 19, 23 UPI/Alamy.com; p. 21 Dmitry Argunov/Shutterstock.com; p. 25 White House/https://en.wikipedia.org/wiki/File:Phoenix_Mercury_at_the_White_House_to_honor_2014_Championship.JPG; p. 29 Chris Poss/Alamy.com.

Printed in the United States of America

Some of the images in this book illustrate individuals who are models. The depictions do not imply actual situations or events.

CPSIA compliance information: Batch #CSGS25: For further information contact Gareth Stevens, New York, New York at 1-800-542-2595.

Find us on

Contents

The True GOAT

GOAT stands for "greatest of all time." To WNBA fans, there's no question about who that is. In fact, in 2021, fans voted and named Diana Taurasi the GOAT of women's basketball! Her incredible accomplishments are unmatched—and she's not done yet!

WHAT A STAR!

The WNBA is the Women's National Basketball Association. Diana is one of the most well-known WNBA players of all time.

Family First

Diana was born June 11, 1982, in California. Her father, Mario, was born in Italy. He met her mother, Liliana, while living in Argentina. Diana has an older sister named Jessika. Spanish was the first language Diana learned! She later learned English and became **bilingual**.

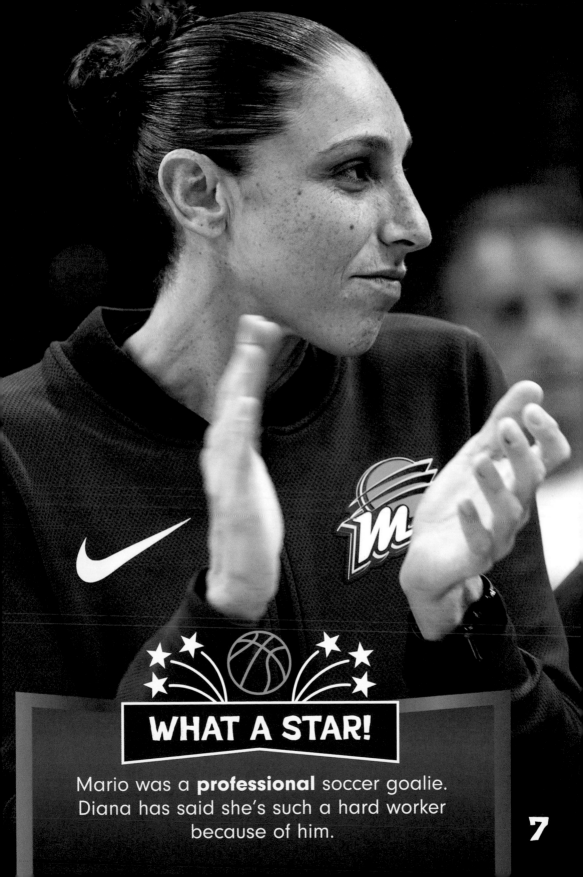

WHAT A STAR!

Mario was a **professional** soccer goalie. Diana has said she's such a hard worker because of him.

Getting on the Court

Diana played both soccer and basketball as a kid. In high school, she started to play basketball more seriously. She scored 3,047 points in high school. That made her one of the highest-scoring young women in California girls' high school basketball history.

WHAT A STAR!

In 2000, Diana was a senior in high school. She was named the girls' basketball high school player of the year.

UConn Huskies

Diana went to the University of Connecticut (UConn) for college. She joined the Huskies women's basketball team. Diana helped lead the Huskies to three back-to-back **championships** in 2002, 2003, and 2004! She was named player of the year in 2003 and 2004 too.

WHAT A STAR!

With Diana, the Huskies didn't lose any of
their 39 games in the 2001–2002 season.
They went on to win 70 games in a row!

A Dream Come True

The WNBA's first season began when Diana was in eighth grade. After going to a game, she knew she wanted to be part of it. This dream came true in 2004. The Phoenix Mercury picked Diana first in the WNBA **draft**!

WHAT A STAR!

Being chosen first in the draft is an honor.
It means Diana was seen as the best player
in the draft that year.

Star from the Start

Diana stood out in her first year. She often led her team in scoring and **assists**. Diana was named the 2004 Rookie of the Year, or the best first-year player. She won this even though the Mercury finished seventh in the WNBA.

PENNY TAYLOR

WHAT A STAR!

Another standout on the Mercury in the 2004 season was Penny Taylor. Diana and Penny got married in 2017! They met when playing for the Mercury.

Olympian

During her first professional basketball season, Diana also took part in the 2004 Olympics in Athens, Greece. That year, the U.S. women's basketball team didn't lose any games! Diana won a gold **medal** with the team after they beat Australia in the finals.

WHAT A STAR!

Other WNBA superstars played on the 2004 Olympic team with Diana, including Sheryl Swoopes, Tina Thompson, Lisa Leslie, and Tamika Catchings.

Mercury Magic

Diana continued to be one of the Phoenix Mercury's leading scorers. Then, in 2007, the team went up against the Detroit Shock in the WNBA Finals. Diana, Penny Taylor, and Cappie Pondexter helped lead their team to the WNBA Championship!

WHAT A STAR!

Diana broke the record for most three-pointers scored in a single WNBA season in 2006 with 121.

Worldwide Star

Diana, like many other WNBA stars, has played in other countries during the WNBA offseason. The teams pay well and help the players stay in shape. Diana has played mostly for teams in Russia and Turkey. She has won the Euroleague Championship six times!

WHAT A STAR!

Diana was named Russian Player of the Year in 2007, 2008, and 2009!

More Medals

Diana returned to the Olympics in 2008 to win another gold medal! She followed that up with three more Olympic gold medals, including one at the Tokyo Olympics held in 2021. Diana was the captain of that team!

WHAT A STAR!

Diana has also played on the USA Basketball Women's Team in the world cup—and won a bronze medal and three gold medals!

MVP

Diana remained at the top in the WNBA. She and the Mercury headed to the WNBA Finals in 2009. The Mercury won the championship again! Diana was named the WNBA MVP, or most **valuable** player. She was named the finals MVP too!

2014 WNBA CHAMPIONS PHOENIX MERCURY WITH PRESIDENT BARACK OBAMA

WHAT A STAR!

Diana won a third WNBA Championship in 2014 with the Mercury. She was named the finals MVP again that year!

Breaking Records

In 2017, Diana made history. She broke Tina Thompson's all-time scoring record! Diana is now the No. 1 all-time scorer in the WNBA. In August 2023, Diana became the first WNBA player to score 10,000 points! She scored 42 points in the game that got her to 10,000.

WHAT A STAR!

Diana accomplished something even greater in 2018. She became a mom for the first time! She and Penny had a son that year.

What's Next?

There's no question Diana is the GOAT! But she hasn't decided to leave the court for good yet. In 2023, she signed with the Mercury for a few more years. There's no telling what else this superstar can accomplish!

WHAT A STAR!

Diana told the *New York Times* in 2020: "I never played for the money. I literally played for the love of the game. I played because I love to compete. I love being on the court."

Diana Taurasi
BY THE NUMBERS

Draft Pick: No. 1

Jersey Number: 3 for the Mercury

Height: 6 feet (1.8 m)

Olympic gold medals: 5
(2004, 2008, 2012, 2016, 2021)

NCAA Championships: 3
(2002, 2003, 2004)

WNBA Championships: 3
(2007, 2009, 2014)

Euroleague championships: 6
(2007, 2008, 2009, 2010, 2013, 2016)

For More Information

BOOKS

Brown, Monica. *Diana Taurasi*. New York, NY: Philomel Books, 2022.

Sabelko, Rebecca. *Diana Taurasi*. Minneapolis, MN: Bellwether Media, 2023.

WEBSITES

Diana Taurasi Stats
www.wnba.com/player/100940/diana-taurasi
Find out more about Diana's career in the WNBA in her player profile.

Official Website of Diana Taurasi
dianataurasi.com/
Check out Diana's official website here.

Glossary

assist: When a player in a sport makes a pass that allows a teammate to score.

bilingual: Able to speak two languages.

championship: The title of the best team in a certain sport.

draft: The process of selecting new players from a pool of possible players entering the league, or group of teams that play together.

medal: A prize given to the winners of a competition. Medals are often made from metal and worn on a ribbon around the neck.

NCAA: National Collegiate Athletic Association, the organization that controls college sports.

professional: Earning money from an activity that many people do for fun.

valuable: Very useful and skilled.

Index